cardboard creations

IN THE HOME

Written by FIONA HAYES

Illustrated by CHRISTIANE ENGEL

Quarto is the authority on a wide range of topics.

Quarto educates, entertains and enriches the lives of our readers—enthusiasts and lovers of hands-on living.

www.quartoknows.com

Author: Fiona Hayes
Illustrations: Christiane Engel
Designers: Starry Dog Books Ltd and Victoria Kimonidou
Editors: Starry Dog Books Ltd and Ellie Brough
Editorial Director: Laura Knowles
Creative Director: Malena Stojic
Publisher: Maxime Boucknooghe

First published in 2019 by QED Publishing,
an imprint of The Quarto Group.
The Old Brewery, 6 Blundell Street,
London, N7 9BH, United Kingdom.
T +44 (0)20 7700 6700
F +44 (0)20 7700 8066
www.QuartoKnows.com

A catalogue record for this book is available from the British Library.

ISBN 978 0 7112 4388 0

Manufactured in Shenzhen, China PP082019
9 8 7 6 5 4 3 2 1

MIX
Paper from
responsible sources
FSC® C001701

The projects in this book are for adults to make. Children should be supervised at all times when in reach of sharp tools. The author and publisher accept no liability for any injuries sustained in making these projects, which are undertaken entirely at your own risk.

CONTENTS

AUTHOR'S NOTE

What can you do with an old cardboard box? You can use it to make something fun to play with!

Small children love to play with an empty box. In their imagination, it quickly becomes a pram, an oven or a washing machine perfect for role-play games.

This book aims to inspire you, the parents or carers, to create a variety of cardboard box items from easily sourced and cheap materials. You get to play with cardboard, glue and paint – hopefully with help from little hands – and your kids get to play with whatever home item you make. Fun all round!

All the models have been gifted to families. I've had lovely photos and some hysterical videos sent back. All have made me smile and some laugh out loud! It's been a delight to see the objects being played with and enjoyed by real children – just as yours will be!

Fiona Hayes

5

GETTING STARTED

Here are a few basic tips and techniques to help you get started on your cardboard creations.

WHERE TO GET BOXES

You can buy large cardboard boxes from removal companies, or look for them in your local free ads – people often give them away after moving house.

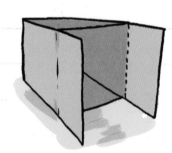

Shops will often give away cardboard boxes for free. For large boxes, try shops selling electrical goods.

Many shops put flattened cardboard boxes out for recycling and, if you ask, will be happy for you to take them away.

YOU WILL NEED

- Cardboard boxes of different shapes and sizes
- Cardboard sheets and offcuts
- Short and long tubes made from thin card
- Narrow tubes made from thick card
- Narrow cardboard canisters (tubes with lids and bases)
- Paper cups and bowls
- Paper straws
- Corrugated cardboard
- Disposable see-through plastic bowls for windows
- Ribbon or string
- Paints
- PVA glue

FOLDING CARDBOARD

1 To fold cardboard, start by placing a ruler where you want the fold to be. Then draw along the edge of the ruler with the end of a closed pen. Press firmly to leave a groove in the cardboard.

2 You can now fold the card along the groove.

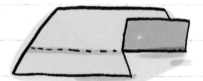

USING A CRAFT KNIFE

Most boxes will be too thick to cut with scissors. For a neat finish, it's best to use a craft knife and metal ruler. The knife is less likely to slip against a metal ruler than a plastic one.

Never allow children to use a craft knife or put their fingers near the blade.

Cut thick cardboard one layer at a time. You may need to make several cuts to get through all the layers.

To cut thick, narrow tubes into lengths, you can use a junior hacksaw or craft knife.

IMPORTANT

Never cut towards the hand that is not holding the knife.

Make sure you always cut away from your free hand.

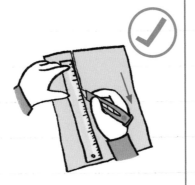

TOP TIP

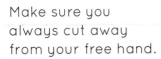

A sharp blade will slice through cardboard without you having to press hard. A blunt blade is likely to slip and cause injury.

CUTTING OPENINGS WITH SCISSORS

Start by drawing the shape of your opening.

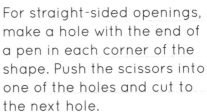

For straight-sided openings, make a hole with the end of a pen in each corner of the shape. Push the scissors into one of the holes and cut to the next hole.

For round openings, make a hole with the end of a pen on the edge of your shape. Push the scissors in to the hole and cut out your shape.

PAINTING AND DECORATING

1 Before you start painting, place a dust sheet or newspaper on the floor so you don't make a mess!

2 Make up all the separate parts of your model and lay them out. Decide what colour to paint them. It's much easier to paint the parts *before* you stick them together.

3 To paint large areas of cardboard, use emulsion tester pots (kids will need adult supervision). To get a good finish, you may need to paint each piece two or three times.

4 Adding strips of painted card to your model can give it a neat finish.

IN THE KITCHEN

Find out how to make a whole kitchen from just a few big boxes. Then add a toaster, mixer, saucepans and vacuum cleaner for more playtime fun!

IT'S WASH DAY!

Make a washing machine that looks just like the real thing. Load it up with smelly socks, shut the door, turn the dial and get washing!

THE MACHINE

1. On the front of the box, cut a round door hinged at one side – see page 15. Cut a large, round hole in the door.

2. Glue in a plastic bowl for a window. Cut a card frame the same size as the door and stick it on to hide the rim of the bowl.

3. Cut a small, bottom-hinged door near the top left corner of the box. Decorate with a strip of corrugated card.

4. Stick a card panel next to the little door.

YOU WILL NEED

- 1 large box
- 1 plastic bowl
- card for door frame and panel
- 1 dial (see page 12)
- corrugated cardboard for decoration
- 1 smaller box for the laundry basket

THE DIAL

Turn to page 12 to make a dial and spindle. Then cut a hole slightly wider than your spindle near the top right corner of the box.

THE LAUNDRY BASKET

To make the laundry basket, turn to page 18.

TEA-TIME DRESSER

A dresser is great for tea parties. You can keep cutlery in the drawers, and put cups, plates and even a yummy cake on the shelves.

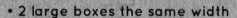
THE CUPBOARD

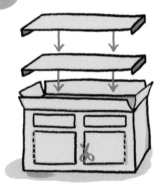

1. Take a large box, and using the doors and windows tutorial on page 15, cut two cupboard doors. Leave enough space above the doors for two drawers.

2. Cut holes for the two drawers.

3. Go to page 30 to make two shelves to go inside the cupboard.

4. Stick one of the shelves inside the box about half way down the door opening.

5. Open up the top flaps and glue the second shelf level with the bottom of the drawer holes.

6. Glue the top flaps together to make the cupboard top.

7. Paint the cupboard.

THE DRAWERS

Turn to page 35 to make the drawers. Paint them the same colour as the cupboard.

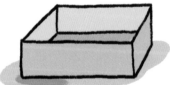

THE HANDLES

Go to page 47 to make handles for the doors and drawers, and glue them on.

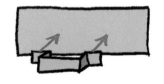

THE TOP SHELVES

1. To make the top shelf unit, cut the back third off a large box and paint it.

2. Using the shelves tutorial on page 30, make two or three shelves and glue them in place as shown.

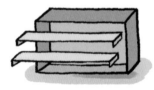

3. Put glue on the bottom of the shelf unit and stick it to the top of the cupboard.

THE SHELF FRONTS

Add strips of cardboard to the fronts of the shelves to give extra strength and to make them look neater.

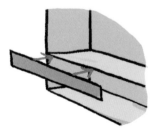

TOP TIP

Paint some paper cups and bowls to put on the shelves.

LET'S GET COOKING!

Make a cooker with an oven door that opens and dials that turn, just like on a real cooker. Then cook up a feast for all your toys!

YOU WILL NEED

- 1 large box
- 10 to 15 cardboard circles at least 35 mm in diameter
- 10 larger circles for the dials
- card for the handle

THE COOKER

1. Using the doors and windows tutorial on page 15, cut a bottom-hinged door in the front of your box. Leave enough space above the door for a row of dials.

2. Cut a window in the middle of the door.

3. Paint your cooker.

THE SHELF

1. Open the top flaps.

2. Go to page 30 to make a shelf. Slide it inside and stick it about half way down the door opening.

3. Glue the top flaps together to make the cooker hob.

THE HANDLE

Turn to page 47 to make a handle for the oven door and stick it on.

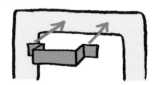

THE DIALS

1. Start by making a spindle for your dial. Cut out two or three cardboard circles and glue them together. For safety, they must be at least 35 mm in diameter. Repeat for each dial.

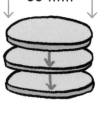
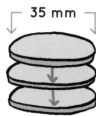

2. Cut out two slightly larger cardboard circles and glue the spindle to one of them, as shown.

3. Cut a row of evenly spaced holes for your dials. The holes should be slightly larger than the spindles.

4. From inside the box, push the spindle through one of the holes.

5. Glue the second large circle to the front of the spindle. Repeat for each of the dials.

ANGLED SIDES

Follow these steps to make an angled box. Cut along the blue dashed lines. Score along the red dashed lines.

1. Open up the end of the box so the flaps stick up.

2. Draw a triangle on the side of the box at the angle you want your object to slope.

3. Cut along two sides of the triangle, leaving it hinged along the edge of the box.

4. Cut off part of the top flap shown here shaded in blue.

5. Cut off the pointed part of the hinged triangle so you are left with a tab that can be used for gluing.

6. Repeat these steps on the opposite side of the box.

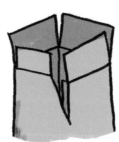

7. The box should now look like this.

8. Score a line along the front of the box level with the bottom of the two gluing tabs.

9. Fold this section in to make the sloping face of your model. Secure it by gluing the two tabs to the inside of the sloping sides.

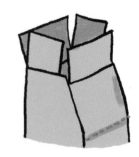

10. Score a line along the top of the sloping face (this part was originally the flap). The score line should be level with the tops of the sloping sides, as shown.

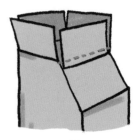

11. Fold the front flap in along the score line – the flap may need trimming to fit the new shorter top. Then fold in the side flaps and finally the back flap, which may need trimming, too. Glue the flaps in place.

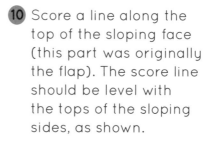
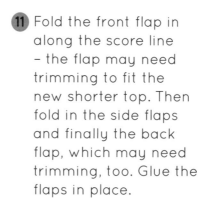

12. For the wheelbarrow, cut off the box below the sloping side, then turn the box over. The flap end forms the base of the wheelbarrow and the top is now open.

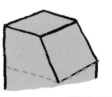

DOORS AND WINDOWS

Find out how to make a rectangular door for the oven and greenhouse, and a round door for the washing machine.

RECTANGULAR

1 Draw your door or window onto the box. For neat rounded corners, draw round a washing-up bowl or jar.

2 Score along the hinge with a pen, then cut along the three opening sides.

3 Open the door outwards.

ROUND

1 Draw a circle on your box where you want your round door to be. Add a straight line for the hinge.

2 Score the hinge with a pen, then cut round the rest of the door and open it outwards.

3 Hold a disposable pudding bowl, rim-side down, against the door, making sure it's in the middle, and draw round it.

4 Cut out the circle, staying a little way inside the line so the hole is slightly smaller than the rim of the bowl.

YOU WILL NEED

- disposable pudding bowl
- cardboard for the frame

5 Push the bowl through the hole and glue the rim to the outside of the window hole.

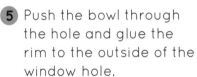

6 Stick a round cardboard frame to the outside of the door to make it stronger and to hide the rim of the bowl.

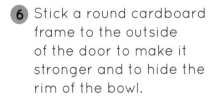

VAC YOUR HOUSE!

Push your vacuum cleaner around the room and pretend to suck up all the dust to leave your house sparkling clean!

YOU WILL NEED

- 1 small box
- 2 short canisters
- 1 short cardboard tube
- 1 long cardboard tube
- 2 wheels (see page 38)

THE BASE AND WHEELS

1. To make the base, angle one side of a small box. Turn to page 14 to find out how.

2. On top of the box, opposite the angled end, cut a hole just big enough to slide the handle through.

3. Turn to page 38 to make two wheels.

4. Place a wheel against the bottom corner of the base and draw round it. In the middle of the circle you've drawn, cut a hole slightly wider than the end of a narrow tube (see page 38). Repeat step 4 on the opposite side of the box.

5. Paint the box.

THE HANDLE

1. Cut the end off a short cardboard tube at a 45 degree angle.

2. Slide the angled end of the short tube over the end of a long tube and glue it in place.

3. Slide the long tube through both holes in the cylinder. Secure by gluing around the holes.

4. Push the end of the long tube into the hole in the base at an angle, and glue it in place.

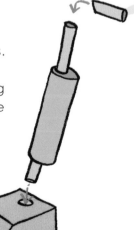

THE CYLINDER

1. Remove the plastic lids from two short canisters and glue the canisters with their open ends together.

2. In the top of the cylinder, near the edge, cut a hole just slightly wider than the handle. Repeat at the other end, making sure the two holes line up. Paint the cylinder.

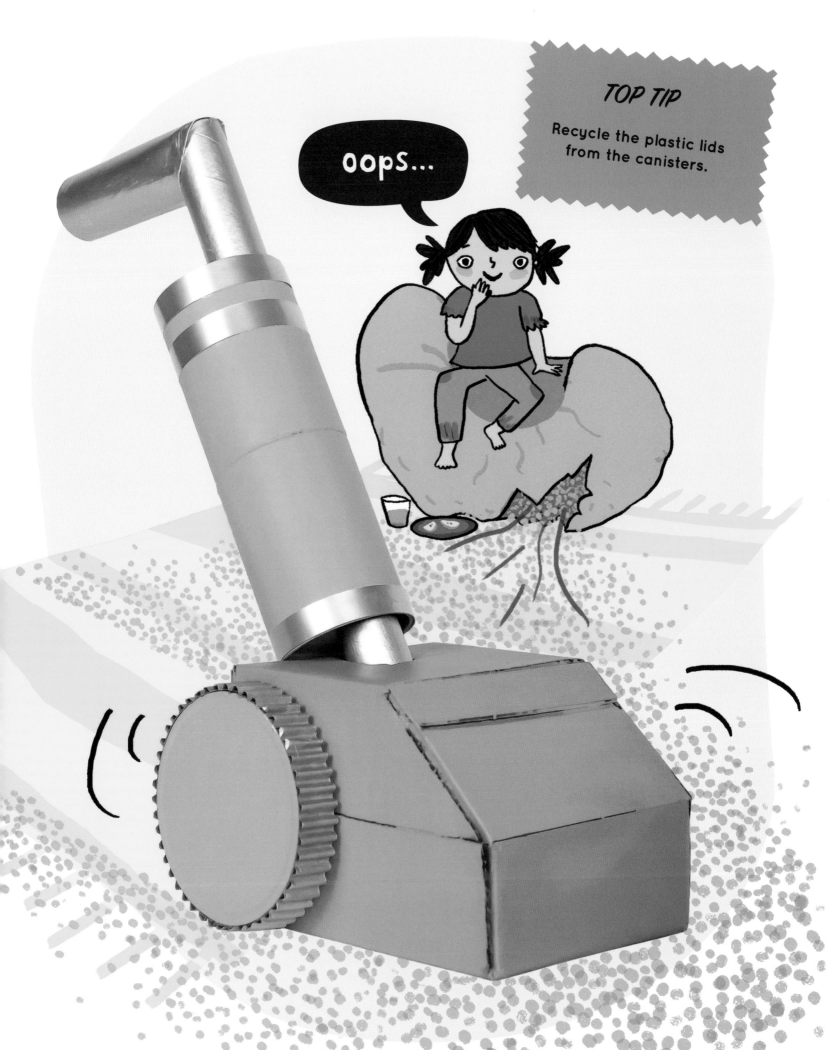

SMALL KITCHEN ITEMS

Make a food mixer, a toaster, some saucepans and a laundry basket to add to your kitchen (photos on page 8).

YOU WILL NEED

FOOD MIXER
• 1 juice carton • 1 tapered box (such as a chocolate box)
• card for circle and mixer tool
• 1 straw • 1 paper bowl or cardboard canister

TOASTER
• 1 small box • card for handle, buttons and bread slices

SAUCEPANS
• paper bowls or cardboard canisters • card for handles

LAUNDRY BASKET
• 1 long box

FOOD MIXER

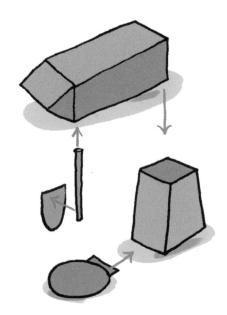

1. Glue a juice carton to the top of a tapered box.

2. Cut out a circle with a side tab from thick cardboard.

3. Glue the tab to the base of the tapered box.

4. Make a mixing tool by gluing a straw to some thick card. Make a hole in the carton, push the end of the straw in and glue in place. Add a mixing bowl.

5. Paint your food mixer.

SAUCEPANS

Cut out a cardboard handle with tab. Glue the tab to the side of a paper bowl or cardboard canister. Paint your saucepans.

TOASTER

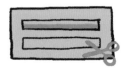

1. Cut two long slots in the top of a small box.

2. Paint your toaster, then add some card buttons and a handle at one end.

3. Cut out some bread-shaped pieces of cardboard. Stick two or three of them together to make thick slices.

THE LAUNDRY BASKET

Cut the two long flaps off the top of a long box. Cut two card handles from the short flaps. Paint your basket.

GOING SHOPPING

Do you love to go shopping? With your own market stall, cash till and trolley you can play shopkeepers all day!

AT THE CHECKOUT

Playing with a cash till is a great way to learn about buying and selling, money and change. Fill your till with coins and get selling!

THE TILL

1. To make the angled front of the till, turn to the tutorial on page 14. Leave enough space to add a drawer at the bottom and a cash display on top.

2. Cut a hole in the front of the box for the drawer.

3. Paint the till.

YOU WILL NEED

- 1 cardboard box
- 1 drawer
- 1 small box
- card for the drawer front, drawer dividers, cash screen, front panel, buttons and coins

THE DRAWER

1. Go to page 35 to make the till drawer.

2. Glue an extra strip of card to the front of the drawer to make it thicker. This will make it easier to pull open. Paint the drawer front.

3. Glue strips of card inside to divide it into sections.

THE BUTTONS

1. Cut out a card panel, paint it and stick it to the sloping front of the till.

2. Add some card circles and squares for buttons.

THE MONEY

Cut out lots of card circles to use as coins. For safety reasons, they must be at least 35 mm in diameter.

THE CASH DISPLAY

Glue a small box to the top of the till for the cash display. Add a card screen.

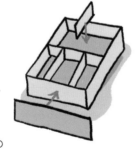

K'ching...!

TOP TIP

Design and make some paper money, too. Draw different pictures for notes of different value!

IT'S MARKET DAY!

Come and buy some lovely bananas! Have fun making all sorts of fruit and vegetables, then sell them from your own market stall.

YOU WILL NEED

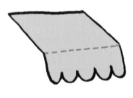

- 1 large cardboard box
- card for shelves
- strips of card for shelf fronts
- 4 uprights
- 4 cardboard strips for the top frame
- 1 canopy
- card for lots of different fruit and vegetables
- cupcake cases

THE STALL

1. Take a large box and cut the front off at an angle.

2. Go to page 30 to make the shelves. Attach them at a slight angle so they slope gently forwards.

3. Use strips of cardboard to make shelf fronts. This will stop the produce sliding off.

THE UPRIGHTS

1. Cut four wide strips of cardboard for the uprights – make the back two slightly longer than the front two.

2. Score the uprights lengthways down the middle and fold each one to make a right angle.

3. At the bottom of each strip, cut a small section from one side.

4. Glue the uprights to the corners of the stall – stick the longer edges to the sides and the shorter edges to the top.

5. Glue four strips of cardboard to the tops of the uprights to make a strong frame.

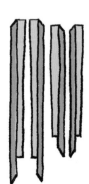
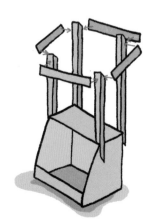

THE CANOPY

Take a large piece of card, score and bend the front edge down, and scallop the edge. Glue the canopy to the top of the frame, so it overhangs the front.

FRUIT AND VEGETABLES

Cut out vegetable and fruit shapes from card and paint them. Cupcake cases make great backs for leafy vegetables (see picture on page 19).

2.00

TOP TIP

You can divide the shelves with narrow strips of cardboard to keep your carrots from your cabbages!

LOAD YOUR TROLLEY

Make a push-along trolley for pretend shopping trips. Imagine filling it with all your favourite goodies!

YOU WILL NEED

- 1 medium-sized box
- 1 narrow cardboard tube
- 4 wheels with axles (see page 38)
- corrugated card for the handle supports

THE BASKET

1. Cut the top off a box at a slight angle along the longest side.

2. On both of the long sides, cut a row of evenly spaced rectangular holes.

3. Leave the short sides solid for strength. Paint the box.

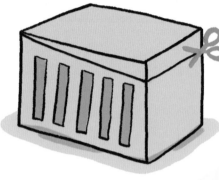

THE WHEELS

Go to page 38 to make two sets of moving wheels, and attach them to the trolley.

THE HANDLE

1. To make the handle, glue a narrow cardboard tube along the top of the tallest end of the box.

2. You can strengthen the handle by gluing strips of corrugated card, smooth side up, over the handle and onto both sides of the trolley.

24

IN THE WORKSHOP

Have fun in your workshop pretending to build your own inventions. Then hang up your tools ready for next time!

BUILD A WORKBENCH

Do you love playing with tools and making things? With this handy workbench, you can keep all your tools in one place.

YOU WILL NEED

- 1 large cardboard box
- 4 long cardboard tubes
- 1 slightly larger box for the worktop and back panel
- strips of stiff card to support the back
- 1 shelf unit (see page 30)

THE BENCH

1. Make two shallow trays by cutting the top and bottom off a large box.

2. Take one of the trays and add legs by gluing a long cardboard tube firmly into each corner.

3. To make the bottom shelf, take the other shallow tray and cut a hole in each corner. Slide the tray onto the legs and glue in place. Turn the bench the right way up.

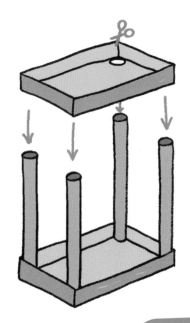

THE TOP SECTION

1. To make the worktop and back panel, cut two adjoining sides from a larger box. Place the hinge along the bench top's back edge and glue one side to the top of the bench.

2. Fold the other side up. To secure it in place, glue long strips of stiff cardboard to the back of the panel and back of the bench.

3. Paint your workbench.

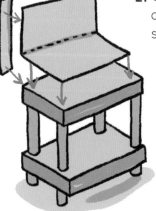

THE SHELF UNIT

1. Go to page 30 to make the shelf unit. Glue it in place.

2. Cut some notches along the front of the shelf to hold the tools.

TOOLBOX AND TOOLS

Saw, hammer and drill your imaginary inventions into shape with this fabulous range of cardboard tools.

THE SCREWDRIVER AND HAMMER

1. Take some thick cardboard and cut out a hammer and screwdriver shape, with tab attached.

2. To make the handles, cut two narrow cardboard tubes to the lengths you want. Push the tabs into the tubes and glue them in.

3. Stick a strip of corrugated card around the top of the screwdriver handle. Paint your tools.

YOU WILL NEED

SCREWDRIVER AND HAMMER
• Thick cardboard • 2 narrow cardboard tubes • corrugated cardboard strip

DRILL
• 1 wide cardboard tube
• 1 medium-wide cardboard tube • 1 short, narrow tube
• corrugated cardboard

TOOLBOX AND MORE TOOLS
• 1 long box • 1 long cardboard tube • thick cardboard

THE DRILL

1. Take a wide cardboard tube and cut a hole in the side near one end.

2. Slide another slightly narrower tube into the hole at a right angle and glue it in place.

3. Stick a card circle to the end of the wide tube, then glue a short, narrow tube to the circle. Add some corrugated card strips to decorate. Paint your drill.

THE TOOLBOX

1. Cut the top off a long box. Cut away the top of each long side.

2. Shape the short sides as shown. Cut a round hole at each end near the top.

3. Slide a long cardboard tube through both holes and glue in place. Paint your toolbox.

MORE TOOLS

To make the spanner, saw, ruler and square rule, cut out the shapes from thick cardboard and paint them.

SHELVES

Find out how to make two kinds of shelves –
open shelves and shelves inside a box.

DRESSER TOP, WORKBENCH TOP

Follow these steps for open shelves.

1 Work out how big the shelves need to be to fit securely. Mark the length and width of the shelf on some cardboard. Allow extra space for tabs on one of the long sides and both of the short sides.

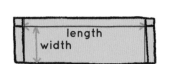

2 Score along the red dashed lines and cut along the blue ones.

3 Fold the tabs up and glue the corner tabs to the insides.

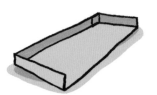

4 For the dresser, turn the shelf over and glue the tabs to the inside of the shelf unit. Use clothes pegs to hold the shelf in place while the glue dries.

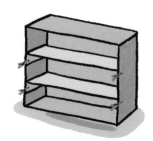

5 For the workbench, cut two pieces of cardboard to make the shelf unit sides. Glue these to either end of the shelves, making sure the shelves are level, then glue the unit in place.

COOKER, DRESSER BASE, GREENHOUSE, MARKET STALL

For shelves inside a box, you may need to open the flaps to put the shelves in, then glue them shut again.

1 Measure how big the shelf needs to be. Mark the length and width of the shelf on some cardboard and cut out the shelf.

2 To make the supports that the shelf will sit on, cut out three 40-mm wide strips of cardboard, as shown.

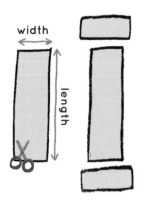

3 Mark where you want the shelf to sit. Glue the support strips just below the mark, on the inside back and adjoining two sides of the model.

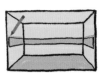

4 Insert the shelf and glue it to the support strips.

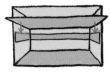

IN THE NURSERY

Take one of your toys for a stroll in her pram, feed her in her high chair, then rock her gently to sleep in her cot!

PUSH-ALONG PRAM

Tuck your dolly into this fabulous push-along pram with wheels that turn. Then take her for a walk to all sorts of imaginary places!

YOU WILL NEED

- 1 medium-sized cardboard box
- 2 cardboard quarter circles
- 3 cardboard struts
- corrugated card for the hood and wheels
- 4 wheels (see page 38)
- 1 handle
- card strips and small circle

THE BASKET AND HOOD

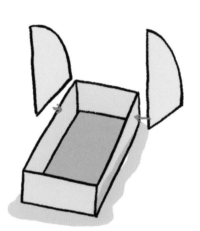

1. To make the pram basket, cut the top off a box. Paint the basket.

2. Next, cut two quarter circle shapes from cardboard for the hood sides. The straight edges should be about half the length of the pram basket.

3. Paint the quarter circles, then glue them to the long sides of the box opposite each other.

4. Cut three long strips of cardboard – they should be slightly longer than the width of the box. Fold the ends over to make a tab at each end. Glue the tabs to the inside edges of the curved hood sides.

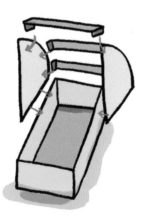

5. Cut a large piece of corrugated cardboard to the same width as the basket. Glue it to the struts and the curved edges of the hood.

6. Decorate the hood with some strips of card and a small circle of card.

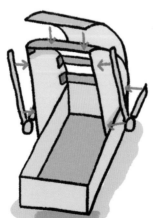

THE HANDLE

Go to page 47 to make the handle for the pram. Paint it and stick it to the end of the basket.

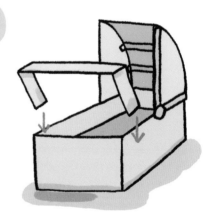

THE WHEELS

To find out how to make and attach two sets of moving wheels, turn to page 38.

TOP TIP

If you have a wide box, you can make a double pram – just right for twins!

ROCK THE CRADLE

Make a cute cardboard cradle for bunny. Wrap her up snug and warm, then sing her a lullaby as you gently rock her to sleep.

THE BASKET

1. Cut the top off a long box, then shape the ends as shown – the ends should be taller than the sides and have curved tops.

2. Cut long, evenly spaced slots along both long sides of the cradle.

3. Paint the cradle.

THE ROCKERS

1. To make the rockers, cut two U-shaped pieces from thick cardboard. The inner curve should be slightly narrower than the end of the cradle, and the outer curve should be slightly wider.

2. Paint the rockers, then stick them to the ends of the cradle low enough that the cradle can rock.

DRAWERS

The dresser and till have real drawers that open, so you can keep things safe inside. Follow these steps to make a drawer.

YOU WILL NEED
• cardboard

1 Work out how big you need the drawer to be so it can easily slide in and out of your model. Start by measuring the length, width and height of the hole it will slide into.

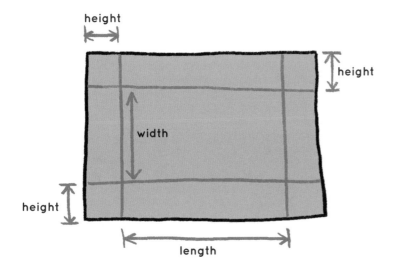

2 Using the guide shown here, and your own measurements, mark out the drawer shape on some cardboard.

3 Score along the red dashed lines and cut along the blue lines.

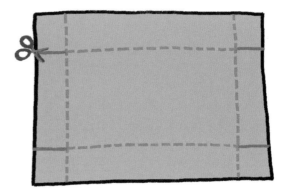

4 Fold the sides up and glue the tabs to the inside to make a box.

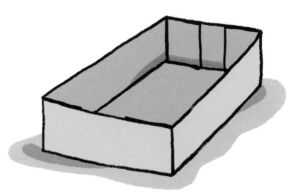

5 Turn to page 47 to find out how to make handles for the dresser drawers.

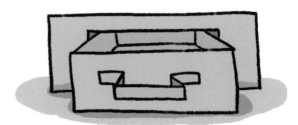

TEDDY'S HIGH CHAIR

Slide teddy into her chair, put on her bib, then cook up some make-believe tea. You can put teddy's bowl on the tray while you feed her.

YOU WILL NEED

- 2 same-size shallow boxes
- 4 long, narrow cardboard tubes
- 1 short, narrow cardboard tube
- thick cardboard for the leg supports and the tray

THE SEAT AND LEGS

1. To make the seat, take a shallow box and cut a round hole in each corner. The holes should be the same width as the cardboard tubes for the legs. Paint the box.

2. Take four long cardboard tubes that are the same length and push one into each hole. They should fit tightly. Glue the tubes in place.

3. Add some narrow strips of cardboard to the legs for extra strength.

4. Paint the chair legs.

THE TRAY

1. Cut out a tray shape from thick cardboard. Fold over the ends to make two tabs, then paint the tray.

2. Cut a round hole near the front edge of the seat and glue in a short cardboard tube – this will support the tray.

3. Glue the tabs of the tray to the back of the chair. Glue the base of the tray to the top of the support tube.

THE CHAIR BACK

To make the chair back, take a box the same size as the seat and paint it. Then glue it to the back edge of the seat.

TOP TIP

Make sure you leave enough space between the tray and the chair back to fit your toy in.

WHEELS

WHEELBARROW

1. Stick a narrow strip of corrugated card around the edge of a round box to look like a tyre.

2. Cut a circle in the middle of the box on both sides, big enough for a cardboard tube to fit through.

3. Cut a short length off a strong, narrow cardboard tube for the axle.

4. Cut two short strips of cardboard, score them in the middle and fold to make a pair of brackets.

5. Push the tube through the holes in the wheel.

YOU WILL NEED

WHEELBARROW
- 1 round box • corrugated cardboard
- 1 short, narrow cardboard tube
- cardboard for brackets

PRAM, TROLLEY, LAWN MOWER
- 1 or 2 long, narrow cardboard tubes
- 1 or 2 wide cardboard tubes
- corrugated card for the tyres
- 2 or 4 round, same-size boxes

VACUUM CLEANER
- 1 long, narrow cardboard tube
- 2 round boxes • corrugated card for the tyres

6. Glue a bracket to each end of the tube.

7. Glue the other ends of the brackets to your wheelbarrow.

PRAM, TROLLEY AND LAWN MOWER

1. Slide a strong, narrow cardboard tube through the middle of a shorter, wider cardboard tube. This is the axle.

2. To make a wheel, stick a narrow strip of corrugated card around the edge of a round box. Repeat.

3. Cut a circle in the middle of one side of the box – make it the same width as the narrow tube.

4. Push both ends of the axle into the wheels and glue.

5. Glue the axle to the base of your model.

VACUUM CLEANER

Make two wheels by following steps 2 and 3 for the Pram, Trolley and Lawn Mower. Push the narrow tube through the holes in the vacuum cleaner body and then push on the wheels and glue them in place.

LET'S GET GARDENING!

Make a fabulous greenhouse, lawn mower, wheelbarrow, tools and potted plants for playtime in the garden!

BUILD A GREENHOUSE

Step inside your own greenhouse and have fun growing little imaginary seeds, or fill it with flowers (see page 46).

(see page 46)

YOU WILL NEED

- 2 large cardboard boxes
- thick cardboard for the shelf and bricks

THE WALLS

1. Take a large box – big enough for a child to stand up in – and cut the top off.

2. Go to the doors and windows tutorial on page 15 to make a door on one side with a small window above it.

3. Cut more windows all round the top half of the box.

4. Paint the window frames and door.

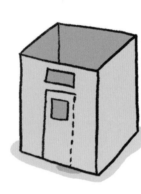

THE SHELF

Go to page 30 to add a shelf inside your greenhouse. You can use this to stand plants on.

THE ROOF

1. Take another large box and cut it in half diagonally. Use one half for the roof.

2. Cut windows on all sides of the roof – if possible, line them up with the windows in the walls.

3. Paint the roof, then glue it to the top of the greenhouse. Use clothes pegs to hold it in place while the glue dries.

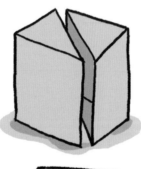

TO DECORATE

1. Cut out lots of rectangles from cardboard and paint them in shades of orange-brown to look like bricks.

2. Glue the card bricks to the sides of the greenhouse in staggered rows.

TOP TIP

If your box is big enough you can add more shelves around the other sides.

WHEEL A BARROW

This push-along wheelbarrow is great for moving plants or tools around the garden. You can even use it for teddy races!

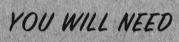

YOU WILL NEED

- 1 large cardboard box
- 2 cardboard tubes for legs
- 2 cardboard tubes for handles
- 1 moving wheel
(see page 38)

THE BARROW

1. Turn to page 14 to find out how to angle one side of your box. The angled side will be the front end of the wheelbarrow.

2. Cut half of the back end off the box.

3. Curve the corners of the sides, at the back end of the box.

THE WHEEL

1. To make the moving wheel, see page 38.

2. Paint the wheel and its bracket, then glue the bracket to the front end of the wheelbarrow.

THE HANDLES

1. Go to page 47 to make two handles. Glue them to the sides at the curved end.

2. Paint your wheelbarrow.

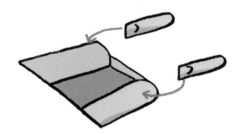

THE LEGS

To make the legs, glue two short lengths of cardboard tube to the base at the curved back end.

PUSH THAT MOWER!

Mowing is good exercise, and nothing smells nicer than freshly cut grass. So get ready to push your mower round the garden!

YOU WILL NEED

- 2 card circles
- 2 paper bowls
- corrugated card
- 1 short, square box
- 4 wheels (see page 38)
- 1 long box
- thick cardboard for the handle

THE MOTOR UNIT

1. For the motor unit, you need two card circles and two paper bowls. Cut the card circles to the same width as the top of the bowls. Paint all the pieces.

2. Glue the circles and bowls together as shown.

3. Glue a strip of corrugated card around the bottom three pieces.

4. Glue the motor unit to the top of a short, square box.

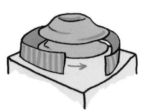

THE GRASS BOX

1. Cut the top off a long box at an angle, leaving the top flap attached at the highest end.

2. Fold the flap down and glue it to the two sloping sides of the box.

3. Glue the short side to the back of the mower body.

THE WHEELS

Go to page 38 and make up two sets of moving wheels. Glue the wheels to the base of the box.

THE HANDLE

Go to page 47 to make a handle from thick cardboard, and attach it to the mower.

TOP TIP

Put some extra pieces of thick cardboard inside the mower body, or the weight of the handle and grass box may make it tip up!

FLOWERS AND TOOLS

Complete your garden and greenhouse with these beautiful flowers in pots, a watering can and a fork and spade.

YOU WILL NEED

FLOWERS
- a variety of egg boxes
- paper straws
- tissue paper
- paper cups

FORK AND SPADE
- cardboard
- 2 handles (see page 47)

WATERING CAN
- 1 oval-shaped cylinder
- 1 short cardboard tube
- cardboard for top and handle

FLOWERS

1. Collect a variety of different-shaped egg boxes to make your flowers. Some have deep bowls and others have tall spikes in between the eggs.

2. Cut out the bowls or spikes, paint them and glue them to paper straws.

3. Glue scrunched-up tissue paper into the centres of the cups, and add some paper leaves.

4. You can use painted paper cups for flower pots.

FORK AND SPADE

1. To make the handles, see page 47.

2. Cut out a fork and spade shape from thick cardboard.

3. On the top edge of each tool cut two slits to make a tab. Slide the tab into the handle and glue it in place.

4. Paint your tools.

WATERING CAN

1. Take an oval-shaped cardboard cylinder and remove the lid. Glue a piece of card over half of the open end.

2. To make the spout, cut a hole in the front of the cylinder and glue in a short cardboard tube at an angle.

3. Add a thick card handle.

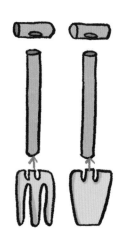

HANDLES

Some models need handles for pushing, others need handles for pulling or lifting. Follow these steps to make four different types of handle.

COOKER, DRESSER

1 Cut a long strip of cardboard. Score and fold the ends to make a wide U shape.

2 Score across the middle of the two end pieces and fold these out to make a right angle.

3 Glue the flattened ends to your model.

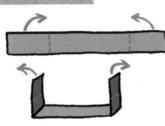

FORK AND SPADE

1 Cut a round hole in a short cardboard tube – make it the same width as the end of a long, narrow tube.

2 Push the long tube into the hole so it fits tightly and glue it in place.

LAWN MOWER, PRAM

1 Cut a long strip of cardboard. Score and fold the ends to make a very long U shape.

2 If the handle is very long, you can add a cross piece, as shown, to give it extra strength.

3 Glue the ends of the handle to your model.

WHEELBARROW

1 Flatten the ends of two cardboard tubes and glue the ends together. You can use pegs to hold everything in place while the glue dries.

2 Glue the flattened ends to your model.

INDEX